Dilemmas and Decisions

Guided/Group Reading Notes

Grey Band

Contents

OXFORD

Introduction

Reading progression in Year 4/Primary 5

By Year 4/P5, the majority of children are developing into confident, capable readers. The focus is on continuing to build their reading fluency and their engagement with reading. Encouraging children to read widely in order to develop personal preferences, critical appreciation and comprehension is central to helping them become enthusiastic readers. Humour, adventure, suspense and identification with interesting characters and intriguing information texts all help create books children look forward to reading. They can sustain independent reading for extended periods of time but chapters and non-fiction spreads offer natural 'break points' for readers who may still find long texts challenging to read. They also create hooks to motivate the reader to want to read further.

Year 4/P5 children recognize most common words on sight. The texts at **grey band** include polysyllabic words and more complex topic based vocabulary. Explicit work on vocabulary continues to be important for improving both reading and writing. Introducing new vocabulary within meaningful contexts helps to extend children's vocabulary range. A wide range of vocabulary, sentence structures and verb tenses is used. Language play (puns, homophones, homonyms, codes, jokes, onomatopoeic words, etc.) can also be found in the texts. Expressive, descriptive and figurative language and vocabulary help create moods and emotions.

In the fiction books, storylines are more complex. Stories are not merely straightforward recounts, but demand inference, deduction and synthesizing of information. The consequences of actions are explored and moral dilemmas that are likely to resonate with children are posed. For example, in the **Dilemmas and Decisions** cluster, *The Witness* explores the issue of being drawn into bullying and *A Matter of Life or Death* looks at real life dilemmas experienced by explorers and adventurers.

The non-fiction books offer examples of a wide range of genres. There are opportunities to compare and contrast different opinions and viewpoints and to evaluate situations and arguments. Texts that contain facts and opinions help children to distinguish between these and help them to respond critically. Factual information is presented in a range of formats.

Visual literacy is supported through the range of visual 'genres' used in the books, for example, comic strips, photo sequences and diagrammatic 'animations'. At grey band, the ratio of text to illustration/photographs is greater, but the illustrations continue to provide additional information and interest for the reader, including opportunities to compare and contrast visual information and source materials. Photos and illustrations *add* to the content and level of reading challenge, rather than simply supporting the text. Visualization comprehension strategies and activities that encourage the reader to reflect on the visual images are suggested in these notes.

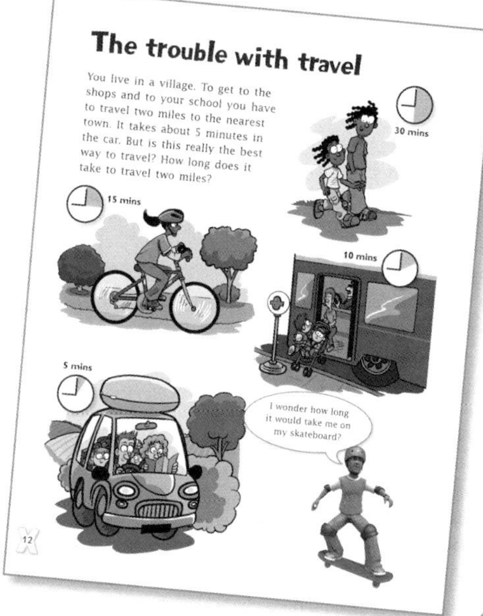

Progression in the Project **X** character books

In this cluster, we gain new insights into the characters – Dr X, Dani Day and Plug and Socket – and the overall plot. In *Making a Stand*, Dr X launches his latest plan to get the watches back from Max, Cat, Ant and Tiger. Dani Day tries to stop him but gets caught, and Plug and Socket decide to rebel. In this book we also find out more about Dr X's life at school and get an indication of why he has grown up to be a super villain. In *The Missing Statue*, Max, Cat, Ant and Tiger decide to investigate the disappearance of the statue of Gladstone Day – Dani Day's father. The reader has to make choices to help solve the mystery … could Dr X be involved?

These two stories help to lead up to a showdown with Dr X in the Great Escapes cluster. Links can also be made to earlier books from brown band: *The Chase* (Fast and Furious), *Heroine in Hiding* (Heroes and Villains), and *The X-bots are Coming ...* and *Attack of the X-bots!* (Strong Defences).

Guided/Group Reading

By Year 4/P5, guided group/reading sessions offer opportunities for children to read independently in a focused way and take part in group discussion to enhance understanding, personal response and an appreciation of the author's craft. There is less of a focus on rehearsing and applying reading cues – although there may be occasions when revisiting these is useful.

These *Guided/Group Reading Notes* provide support for each book in the cluster, along with suggestions for follow-up activities. Books in the grey band can be covered in around three guided/ group reading sessions. Alternatively, children may read much of each book in grey band independently and only undertake one or two guided/group reading sessions around the text. Although guided/group reading suggestions for all of the book are given under each section of the notes, teachers can select which chapters/non-fiction spreads they wish to use in guided/ group reading sessions.

Speaking, listening and drama

Talk continues to be crucial to learning at this stage. At Year 4/P5, children still need plenty of opportunities to express their ideas through talk and drama, and to listen to and watch the ideas of others. These processes are important for building reading engagement, personal response, confidence, and understanding and for rehearsing some writing possibilities. Suggestions for speaking, listening and drama are provided for every book. Within these *Guided/Group Reading Notes* the speaking and listening activities are linked to the reading assessment focuses.

Building comprehension

Understanding what we have read is at the heart of reading.
To help readers become effective in comprehending a text these
Guided/Group Reading Notes contain practical strategies to
develop the following important aspects of comprehension:

- Previewing
- Predicting
- Activating and building prior knowledge
- Questioning
- Recall
- Visualizing and other sensory responses
- Deducing, inferring and drawing conclusions
- Determining importance
- Synthesizing
- Empathizing
- Summarizing
- Personal response, including adopting a critical stance.

The research basis and rationale for focusing on these aspects of
comprehension is given in the *Teaching Handbook* for Year 4/P5.

Reading fluency

Reading fluency combines automatic word recognition, reading
with pace, and expression. Rereading, fluency and building
comprehension support each other. This is discussed more
fully in the *Teaching Handbook*
for Year 4/P5. Opportunities for
reading aloud are important in
building fluency, and reading
aloud to children provides them
with models of expressive fluent
reading. Suggestions for purposeful
and enjoyable oral reading and
rereading/relistening activities are
given in the follow-up activities to
guided/group reading and in the notes
for parents. It is worth noting that
rereading activities do not have to be
undertaken immediately after a book
has been read.

The Project X *Interactive Stories* software can be used to provide a model of reading fluency for the whole class and/or opportunities for individuals or small groups of children to listen to stories again and again. Listening to stories being read is particularly effective with EAL children. The grey band story *Making a Stand* is on the *Interactive Stories* CD-ROM for Year 4/P5.

Building vocabulary

Explicit work on enriching vocabulary is important in building reading fluency and comprehension (see the section on vocabulary building in the *Teaching Handbook* for Year 4/P5). By Year 4/P5, children have a familiar core vocabulary. Reading is the most important means by which children encounter new vocabulary once this core of everyday oral vocabulary is established. However, further work needs to be undertaken if newly encountered written words are to become part of the child's vocabulary repertoire. Suggestions for vocabulary work are included in these notes. The vocabulary chart on pages 10–11 shows new or challenging vocabulary introduced in each book. Reusing these words orally or in their own writing helps these words become established. The chart also indicates those words that can be used to support learning alongside a structured spelling programme.

Developing a thematic approach

Helping children make links in their learning supports their development as learners. All the books in this cluster focus on the theme **Dilemmas and Decisions**. A chart showing the cross-curricular potential of this theme is given in the *Teaching Handbook* for Year 4/P5, along with a rationale for using thematic approaches. Some suggestions for cross-curricular activities are also given in these notes, in the 'Follow-up activities' suggestions for each book.

In guided/group reading sessions, you will also want to encourage children to make links between the books in the cluster. Grouping books in a cluster allows readers to make links between characters, events, actions and information across the books.

This enables readers to build complex understandings of characters and information gradually, to give reasons why things happen and how characters may change and develop. It can help them recognize cause and effect. It helps children reflect on the skill of determining importance, as a minor incident or detail in one book may prove to have greater significance when considered across several books.

Note that the books in this cluster can be read in any order.

In the **Dilemmas and Decisions** cluster, some of the suggested links that can be explored across the books include:

- weighing up evidence and arriving at a reasoned decision
- examining shared vocabulary, including the use of modal verbs (could, might, etc.) to indicate tentativeness and the potential for alternative possibilities.

Reading into writing

The Project X books provide both writing models and inspiration to support children's writing. Brief suggestions for relevant, contextualized and interesting writing activities are given in the follow-up activities for each book. These include both short and longer writing opportunities. The activities cover a wide range of writing contexts so children can develop an understanding of adapting their writing for different audiences and purposes.

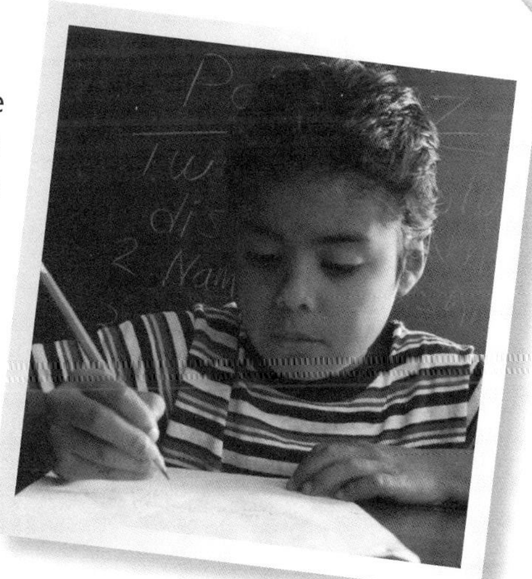

The Project X *Interactive Stories* software contains a collection of 'clip art' assets from the character books that children can use in their writing.

Selecting follow-up activities

These *Guided/Group Reading Notes* give many ideas for follow-up activities. Some of these can be completed within the guided/group reading session. Some are longer activities that will need to be worked on over time. You should select those activities that are most appropriate for your pupils. It is not expected that you would complete all the suggested activities.

Home/school reading

Books used in a guided/group reading session can also be used in home/school reading programmes.

Before a guided/group reading session, the child could:
- read specified chapters or sections of a book
- read a related book from the cluster or elsewhere to build background knowledge.

Following a guided/group reading session, the child could:
- reread the book at home to build reading confidence and fluency
- read the next chapter/s or section/s
- read a related book from the cluster.

Advice for parents on supporting their child with reading at home is provided inside individual books. There is further advice for teachers concerning home/school reading partnerships in the *Teaching Handbook* for Year 4/P5.

Assessment

During guided/group reading, teachers make ongoing reading assessments of individuals and of the group. Reading targets are indicated for each book and you should assess against these reading targets. You should select just one or two targets at a time as the focus for the group. The same target can be appropriate for several literacy sessions or over several texts.

Readers should be encouraged to self-assess and peer-assess against the target/s.

Further support for assessing pupils' progress is provided in the *Teaching Handbook* for Year 4/P5.

 ## Continuous reading objectives and ongoing assessment

The following objective will be supported in *every* guided/group reading session and is therefore a continuous focus for attention and assessment (AF3). This objective is not listed in full for each book but as you listen to individual children discussing their reading you should undertake ongoing assessment, against this objective:

- Interrogate texts to deepen and clarify understanding and response **8.2**

Further objectives are provided as a focus within the notes for each book, as appropriate, from these strands:

- Word structure and spelling (*Strand 6*)
- Understanding and interpreting texts (*Strand 7*)
- Engaging with and responding to texts (*Strand 8*).

Correlation to specific objectives within the Scottish, Welsh and Northern Ireland curricula are provided in the *Teaching Handbook* for Year 4/P5.

 ## Recording assessment

The assessment chart for the **Dilemmas and Decisions** cluster is provided in the *Teaching Handbook* for Year 4/P5.

 ## Diagnostic assessment

If an individual child is failing to make good progress, or he or she seems to have a specific problem with some aspect of reading, you will want to undertake a more detailed assessment. Details of how to use running records for diagnostic assessment and resource sheets for undertaking such assessments are given in the *Teaching Handbook* for Year 4/P5.

Vocabulary chart

At Year 4/P5, children should:

- read most words independently and automatically
- distinguish the spelling and meaning of common homophones
- know and apply common spelling rules
- develop a range of personal strategies for learning new and irregular words.

NB Examples only given in each category.

The Missing Statue	Homophones	been, tyre, wait, hire, way, there
	Spelling rule: Adding 'ing' For most words just add 'ing'	thinking, looking, pointing, going, hanging, zooming
	New and irregular context words	instructions, statue, plinth, investigating, laser, reception, laboratory equipment
Making a Stand	Homophones	pair, four, two, there
	Spelling rule: Adding 'ing' The consonant is doubled if the word ends in short vowel + consonant e.g. sit/sitting	humming, grinning, tapping
	New and irregular context words	security, codes, dilemma, elite, tunnel, position, decisions, defiantly

It's Your Call	Homophones	waste, which, for
	Spelling rule: Adding 'ing' 'e' is dropped at the end of a word when 'ing' is added, e.g. make/making	rising, living, deciding, cycling
	New and irregular context words	pollution, environment, droughts, technology, vehicles, campaign, devastating, generations, atmosphere, emissions, electricity, renewable
The Witness	Homophones	whether, which, waste, to, ate, there
	Spelling rule: Adding 'ing' 'y' at the end of a word does not usually change when 'ing' is added	bullying (compare this with bullied, bullies)
	New and irregular context words	cavalry, diabetes, bullying, trampoline, lemonade, epidemic, injection, citizenship, collection box, insulin, temperature, disappointed, victim, counselling
A Matter of Life and Death	Homophones	sea, four, right, which, two, no, their, new, would
	Spelling rule: Adding 'ing' 'e' is dropped at the end of a word when 'ing' is added, e.g. make/ making	navigating, living, using, gazing, shaving, surviving, racing, including, freezing
	New and irregular context words	navigate, decision, explorer, mutiny, sextant, buccaneer, ammunition, transmitter, expedition, resourceful, endurance, uninhabited, hazard

The Missing Statue

BY ALEX LANE

About this book

A statue of the famous scientist, Gladstone Day, has been stolen from the park. The friends pair up to follow different clues, but both routes lead them to NASTI headquarters and another encounter with Dr X, Plug and Socket and the X-bots.

You will need

- *Story flow diagram* Photocopy Master I, *Teaching Handbook* for Year 4/P5

- *Character logs* Photocopy Master, *Teaching Handbook* for Year 4/P5

- *Vocabulary detectives* Photocopy Master, Teaching Handbook for Year 4/P5

	Literacy Framework objective	Target and assessment focus
Speaking, listening, group interaction and drama	o Tell stories effectively and convey detailed information coherently for listeners 1.3	o We can enact and retell the story we have read **AF2/3**
Reading See also continuous reading objectives listed on page 9.	o Identify and summarize evidence from a text to support a hypothesis **7.1** o Interrogate texts to deepen and clarify understanding and response **8.2** o Use knowledge of word structures and origins to develop their understanding of word meanings **7.4**	o We can identify clues to a character's personality and justify our ideas with evidence from the text **AF2/3** o We can answer questions and discuss what we have read **AF2/3** o We can identify vocabulary on the theme of detection and say what the words mean **AF2**

This book has a non-linear structure. There is a shared opening (pp.3–5) and ending (pp. 42–48). Children can choose one of two routes through this story – Route 1: to go with Max and Tiger, or Route 2: to go with Cat and Ant. Readers will be asked different questions depending on the route selected. The following notes provide three guided/group reading sessions. They can be used flexibly; you may choose to focus on all three sessions or you could focus on one session and have the children read the rest of the book independently.

In Session 1, children read the shared opening and select a route. They will follow their route and stop reading at page 20 or 23 (Route 1) or page 25 (Route 2). In Session 2 children following Route 1 will read to page 39, those following Route 2 will read to page 41. (Routes converge on page 42). In Session 3 children will read the shared ending (pp.42–48).

Session 1

Before reading

To activate prior knowledge and encourage predicting

- Look at the front cover and discuss the likely story line. **(predicting)**
- Read page 2 together and find an example of each kind of instruction box in the book. Check that children understand what to do when they encounter such a box.

To engage readers and model fluent reading

- Get one child to read page 3 in the style of a newsreader.
- How does the statue link with the ongoing story/characters? **(deducing, inferring)**
- Have they met Inspector Textor before? If so, where? **(recall, activating prior knowledge)**

During reading

- Ask the children to read to the end of page 5 and decide which pair of friends they will follow. If they select Route 1 they should read to the end of page 23; if they choose Route 2 they should read to the end of page 25.
- As they read, ask them to think about clues the children find and what these show. **(deducing, inferring, drawing conclusions)**

··>

Assessment point

Listen to individual children reading and make ongoing assessments on their decoding, sight vocabulary, approaches to tackling new words and their reading fluency. AF1

After reading

Returning to the text

Ask all the children:

- Why is Gladstone Day a hero for Ant? What does it tell us about Ant's interests/personality? **(recall, inferring)**

Ask Route 1 children:

- Where do Max and Tiger follow the tracks to? **(recall)**
- Where do they think the statue is? **(predicting)**

Ask Route 2 children:

- Why do Ant and Cat shrink? **(inferring)**
- How do they know someone has been in the den? **(deducing)**
- How do they escape the X-bot? **(recall)**

Building comprehension

- Use the *Story flow diagram* Photocopy Master to plot significant events so far. Enlarge this to A3 if possible. The story can be plotted in words or pictures or both. Once the diagram is completed, highlight points where any of the characters has to make a decision. **(visualizing, determining importance, summarizing)**

- Use the *Character log* Photocopy Master to record evidence of the children's characters. **(drawing conclusions, personal response)**

> **Assessment point**
>
> Can children use evidence from the text to gain understanding about the characters? AF2/3

Building fluency

- Ask children to enact the scene on pages 4–5, encouraging them to think about the expressions, tone of voice and gestures to use, guided by words such as *fumes, scoffs, hopefully,* and actions such as 'scratches his head'. **(empathy)**

Building vocabulary

- Ask the children to note down any words to do with detecting, e.g. investigating (p.5), on the *Vocabulary detectives* Photocopy Master. Ask them to try to find the meanings of any unfamiliar words.

> **Assessment point**
>
> Can children identify the themed vocabulary and say what it means? AF2

 Before reading

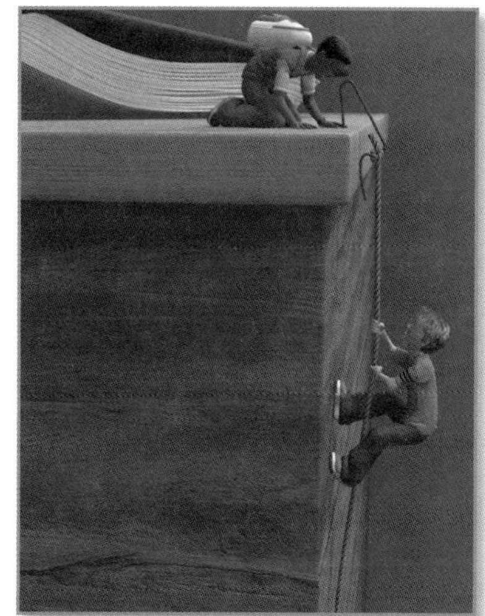

To activate prior knowledge and encourage predicting

- Recap the story to date, discussing the different routes and how various characters are feeling. **(recall)**
- What have the children learnt from the pictures as well as from the text? **(deducing, inferring)**

During reading

- Ask Route 1 children to read the 'Move on' box on page 23 and continue reading to page 39; Route 2 children read the 'Move on' box on page 25 and continue reading to the end of page 41.
- As they read, ask them to think about the different decisions the children have to make.

> **Assessment point**
>
> Make ongoing assessments on children's decoding, sight vocabulary, approaches to tackling new words and their reading fluency. AF1

 After reading

Returning to the text

Ask Route 1 children:

- How do Max and Tiger manage to 'follow' Plug and Socket? **(recall)**
- What does Plug and Socket's desire for ice cream tell you about their character? **(inferring)**
- Why does Dr X want the secrets about micro technology? **(deducing)**

Ask Route 2 children:

- What changes has Ant made to the micro-buggy? (p.28) Why? **(recall)**
- Why does Cat take the micro-buggy downstairs? (p.36) **(inferring)**
- What do you think Ant's idea is? (p.41) **(predicting)**

Building comprehension

- Continue the *Story flow diagram* Photocopy Master of the route to this point to plot significant events. Highlight points where the characters have to make a decision. **(visualizing, determining importance, summarizing)**

- Start or continue to use the *Character log* Photocopy Master to record evidence of one of the characters. **(drawing conclusions, personal response)**

> **Assessment point**
>
> Can children continue to use evidence from the text to gain understanding of the characters? AF2/3

Building fluency

- Ask children to enact the scene inside NASTI (p.38). Ask them to think about the expressions, tone of voice and gestures to use, guided by their understanding of the characters involved. **(empathy)**

> **Assessment point**
>
> Can children enact and retell the story effectively? AF2

Session 3

Before reading

To activate prior knowledge and encourage predicting

- In pairs, ask the Route 1 children to outline their story so far to the Route 2 children, and then swap roles. **(recall, summarizing)**

During reading

- Ask Route 1 children to read the 'Move on' box on page 39, and Route 2 children to read the 'Move on' box on page 41, before reading to the end.

- As they read, ask them to think about how Ant must be feeling during this section of the plot. **(empathy)**

> **Assessment point**
>
> Listen to individual children reading and make ongoing assessments on their decoding, sight vocabulary, approaches to tackling new words and their reading fluency. AF1

After reading

Returning to the text

- How does Gladstone Day's invention become important? **(recall)**
- What personal qualities does Ant demonstrate? **(inferring, empathy)**
- Which adventure was the most exciting and why? **(personal response)**

Building comprehension

- Start or continue the *Story flow diagram* Photocopy Master to plot significant events. Highlight points where any of the characters have to make a decision. **(visualizing, determining importance, summarizing)**
- Start, continue to use or complete the *Character log* Photocopy Master to record evidence of one of the characters. **(drawing conclusions, personal response)**

> **Assessment point**
>
> Have the children formed an accurate picture in their minds of the characters' personalities? AF2/3

Building fluency

- Ask one child to read page 48 in the style of a newsreader.

Building vocabulary

- Ask the children to add further words to do with detecting to their *Vocabulary detectives* Photocopy Master, finding and adding meanings of any unfamiliar words.

> **Assessment point**
>
> Can children identify vocabulary on the theme of detection and say what the words mean? AF2

Follow-up activities

Writing activities

- Compare the two newspaper articles and identify the features.
- Write a newspaper article about the sighting of a fast-moving miniature buggy on the High Street. **(longer writing task)**
- Create non-linear stories that have a shared beginning and ending but different routes through the story. **(longer writing task)**
- Write a brief police report on the missing statue. **(short writing task)**

Other literacy activities

- Create an outside broadcast report from the site of the missing/returned statue. **(speaking and listening)**

Cross-curricular and thematic opportunities

- Create a maths board game that involves making decisions at certain points on the board. **(Maths)**
- Look at examples of local statues. Investigate who they are and why they are famous. **(History)**
- Look at the work of famous sculptors, particularly work on human forms. Create mini statues using wire. **(Art and design)**

Making a Stand

BY TONY BRADMAN

About this book

At NASTI headquarters, Dani looks on in horror as an army of X-bots sets off to capture the watches. She tries to warn the children but is captured and brought to Dr X. As the story ends, Dani escapes knowing she must help the children.

You will need

- *Talking frame* Photocopy Master 2, *Teaching Handbook* for Year 4/P5
- *Character logs* Photocopy Masters, *Teaching Handbook* for Year 4/P5
- *Vocabulary detectives* Photocopy Master, *Teaching Handbook* for Year 4/P5
- *I think, I say, I feel* Photocopy Master, *Teaching Handbook* for Year 4/P5

	Literacy Framework objective	**Target and assessment focus**
Speaking, listening, group interaction and drama	o Create roles showing how behaviour can be interpreted from different viewpoints **4.1**	o We can role play Dr X showing different aspects of his life and character, using appropriate language **AF2/3**
Reading See also continuous reading objectives listed on page 9.	o Identify and summarize evidence from a text to support a hypothesis **7.1** o Interrogate texts to deepen and clarify understanding and response **8.2** o Explain how writers use figurative and expressive language to create images and atmosphere **7.5**	o We can identify clues to a character's personality and justify our ideas with evidence from the text **AF2/3** o We can answer questions and discuss what we have read **AF2/3** o We can identify how language is used to create images and atmosphere **AF2/5**

This book has a structure of three parallel subplots, which come together in the final chapter. The following notes provide a structure for up to three guided/group reading sessions. They are intended to be used flexibly; you may choose to focus on all three sessions or you could focus on one session and have the children read the rest of the book independently. In Session 1, children will read Chapter 1. Chapter 2 should be read independently before Session 2. In Session 2 they will read Chapter 3, with Chapter 4 being read independently. In Session 3 they will read Chapter 5 – the final chapter.

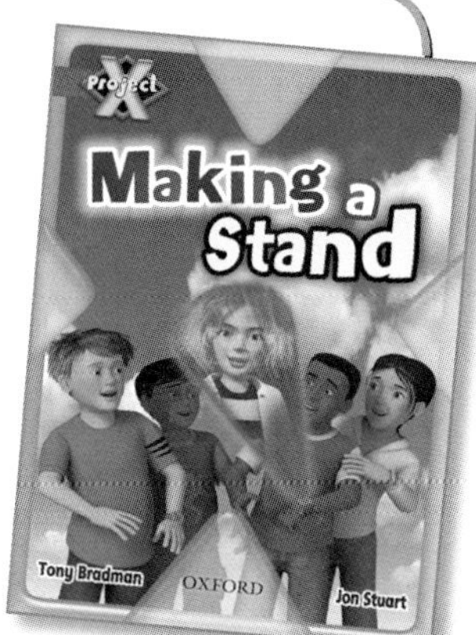

Session 1 (Chapter 1)

 **Before reading**

To engage readers and support fluent reading

- Talk about the title 'Making a Stand'. Ask children what they think the phrase means.

- Ask children who might be making a stand against Dr X. Why?

- Ask the group to recall interactions between Dr X, Plug and Socket in other books. How does the way they talk to each other differ? How has the relationship changed since childhood? **(recall, inferring, deducing)**

- Tell the children that they will see a change in the relationship between these characters in this book. First they will meet Dani again.

- Look at the chapter heading together and discuss what 'elite' means.

During reading

- Ask the children to read the first chapter. As they read, ask them to note down words and phrases that build tension, e.g. *river of shiny black chrome* (p.7), *shuddered* (p.8).

· ·>

Assessment point

Listen to individual children reading and make ongoing assessments on their decoding, sight vocabulary, approaches to tackling new words and their reading fluency. AF1

 ## After reading

Returning to the text

- Why is Dr X's smile 'satisfied' on page 4? **(recall, inferring)**
- What do the X-bots have to do? (p.6)
- Why did Dani shudder and watch in horror? (p.8) **(empathy, inferring, and deducing)**
- What is Dani's dilemma? How does she solve it? (pp.13–15)
- How does the author build tension at different points in the chapter, including the ending?

> **Assessment point**
>
> Can children interrogate the text, showing understanding and giving personal responses to it? AF2/3

Building comprehension

- Ask the children, in pairs, to retell the chapter as though they were Dani, using the *Talking frame* Photocopy Master. Each child takes a turn to tell the story in the first person to their partner. Go through the *Talking frame* with them, ensuring they understand how it relates to the chapter. Encourage them to talk about how they felt, what they saw and did. **(recall, deducing, inferring, empathizing)**

- Give the children five minutes to prepare their talk. Ask the listening partner to say one thing they think the talker did well and one thing that could be improved upon. The criteria listed on the *Talking frame* will help. **(peer assessment)**

- Use the *Character log* Photocopy Master to record evidence on the main characters in this chapter – Dr X, Dani, Plug and Socket. **(drawing conclusions, personal response)**

> **Assessment point**
>
> Can children use evidence from the text to gain understanding about the characters? AF2/3

Building vocabulary

- Discuss some of the tension words and phrases the children found in the chapter. Using the *Vocabulary detectives* Photocopy Master, ask the children to add all the tension words and phrases around the picture on page 9.

- Ask children to read Chapter 2 independently before the next session.

 **Before reading**

To activate prior knowledge and encourage prediction

- Recap the story to date. Ask a few questions about Chapter 2, which has been read independently.
- Why do Plug and Socket decide they have had enough?
- Why do they feel brave enough to tackle Dr X?

 **During reading**

- Ask the children to read Chapter 3. As they read, ask them to look out for clues that show that the friends don't always get on.

Assessment point

Listen to individual children reading and make ongoing assessments on their decoding, sight vocabulary, approaches to tackling new words and their reading fluency. AF1

 **After reading**

Returning to the text

- How does the author create the atmosphere in the first sentences of the chapter? What double meaning is there in 'as if a storm was coming'? Where does the author use words to create tension?

Assessment point

Can children identify how language is used to create images/atmosphere? AF2/5

- What evidence did they find of the friends not getting on?
- Why are the friends 'truly scared' for the first time? (p.30)
- How does Max show leadership? (p.31)
- What is the effect of the repeat cliffhanger in Chapters 2 and 3?

Assessment point

Can children interrogate the text, showing understanding and giving personal responses to it? AF2/3

Building comprehension

- Use the *Character log* Photocopy Master to record evidence of the characters. **(drawing conclusions, personal response)**

- Plot the structure of this chapter – (small fall out, Dani's message, big fall out, Max's decisions). Discuss why the author puts in the minor disagreements at the start of the chapter. **(summarizing)**
- Ask children to enact the moments when the message gets through, freeze framing when they come to the word, *danger*. Use questioning and record what the four friends think, say and feel on the *I think, I say, I feel* Photocopy Master. **(empathy)**
- Ask children to read Chapter 4 independently before the next session.

Session 3 (Chapter 5)

Before reading

To activate prior knowledge and encourage predicting:
- Recap the story to date, asking questions about Chapter 4, which the children have read independently. **(recall, summarizing)**
- How and where does the author use humour?
- Why does Dr X say, "So, we meet again Miss Day"?
- How do the X-bots know where Dani, Plug and Socket are?

During reading

- Ask the children to read Chapter 5, to the end of the book. As they read, ask them to think about why Dr X is feeling confident. What attributes does he think make him successful?

After reading

Returning to the text
- Where does the chapter 'turn' and Dr X begin to seem less successful?
- What phrases/actions make the friends seem vulnerable?
- What do they think of the cliffhanger ending?

Assessment point
Can children interrogate the text, showing understanding and giving personal responses to it? AF2/3

Building comprehension
- Add evidence about the characters to the *Character log* Photocopy Master. **(drawing conclusions, personal response)**

- Make a story board showing the main events of this chapter and the point at which the chapter 'turns' from a triumph to a disaster for Dr X. **(visualization, summarizing)**

....>

- Allocate three children to be Dr X, Plug and Socket. Ask the children to stay in role and invite the other children to question them about their life together as young people. **(questioning)**

....>

Follow-up activities

Writing activities

- Write a play script using the storyboard from Session 3. Use the clip art from the Project X *Interactive Stories* to turn the storyboard into a presentation, acting out the script, and recording it. Music could be added. **(longer writing task, drama)**
- Use the first person activity from Session 1 as a model for turning other scenes into first person accounts. Children can create their own talking prompt frames using the book. Move from talk into writing. **(speaking and listening, longer writing task)**
- Reread page 18 about Plug's expectations when he joined NASTI. Create a job advertisement for a henchman to Dr X. **(short writing task)**

Cross-curricular and thematic opportunities

- Research what a comet is and create fact files on famous comets such as Halley's Comet and Hale Bop. **(Science, ICT)**
- Discuss the dilemmas and decisions involved in computer security versus computer freedom. What are sensible rules for staying safe on the Internet? **(PSHE, ICT)**

It's Your Call

BY HAYDN MIDDLETON

About this book

This non-fiction persuasive text discusses how the increase in use of technology and the rising world population is causing a depletion of the Earth's resources. It poses questions for readers to consider ways they can tackle this dilemma on a personal level. The book also covers up-to-date topics such as global warming and alternative fuel sources.

You will need

- *It's Your Call summary* Photocopy Master 3, *Teaching Handbook* for Year 4/P5

- *It's Your Call writing frame* Photocopy Master 4, *Teaching Handbook* for Year 4/P5

	Literacy Framework objective	**Target and assessment focus**
Speaking, listening, group interaction and drama	o Offer reasons and evidence for their views, considering alternative opinions 1.1 o Respond appropriately to the contributions of others in the light of differing viewpoints 1.2	o We can debate issues and reach a decision, listening to and responding to different views **AF2/3**
Reading See also continuous reading objectives listed on page 9.	o Use knowledge of different organizational features of texts to find information effectively **7.3** o Identify and summarize evidence from a text to support a hypothesis **7.1**	o We can locate information efficiently and use it to support our ideas **AF2**

The following notes provide a structure for up to three guided/group reading sessions. They are intended to be used flexibly; you may choose to focus on all three sessions or you could focus on one session and have the children read the rest of the book independently. In Session 1, children will read pages 2–11. In Session 2 they will read a section of their own choosing. In Session 3 children will read pages 21–27 and page 30. Sections not read during guided/group reading sessions should be read independently.

Session 1 (pages 2–11)

 ### Before reading

To activate prior knowledge and encourage prediction

- Look at the front cover and discuss what the phrase 'It's Your Call' means. **(activating prior knowledge)**
- Looking at the front cover and the contents page, what kind of issues do the children think they will be asked to form an opinion about? **(prediction)**
- Look at the words in bold on pages 2–3 and check that children understand their meaning. Use the glossary to confirm or supplement their explanations.

To engage readers and model fluent reading

- Ask some of the children to read pages 2 and 3 aloud to the rest of the group.
- Ask each child to respond to this page with his or her immediate thoughts and feelings. **(personal response)**

During reading

- Ask the children to read pages 4–11.
- If you have not already done so, ask the children what to do if they encounter a difficult word, modelling with an example from the book if necessary, e.g. agricultural (p.18).
- As they read, ask them to think about their personal answers to the questions in the 'It's Your Call' boxes on pages 7 and 11.

> **Assessment point**
>
> Listen to individual children reading and make ongoing assessments on their decoding, sight vocabulary, approaches to tackling new words and their reading fluency. **AF1**

 **After reading**

Returning to the text

- Have a brief discussion about the children's immediate thoughts and feelings on these topics and their response to the 'It's Your Call' boxes.
(personal response)

- Ask all children to use the index to locate the answers in the text, to these questions:

- What is a landfill site?

- How do charities recycle mobile phones?

- How could you use a washing machine less often?

Building comprehension

- Ask children to make brief notes about the information in the text, for example, using three bullet points under each of these headings: 'Why we should recycle'; 'Why we should save water'. Ask them to look for facts (not opinions) to support these views. They will return to these notes and add to them in subsequent readings. Demonstrate how children can combine facts from different pages together, e.g. as the population is rising to nine billion, and technology allows us to use more water than ever before, demand will continue to rise. **(synthesizing, inferring, deducing)**

> **Assessment point**
>
> Can they locate information efficiently and use it to support a point of view? **AF2**

Building vocabulary

- Look at the word 'uninhabitable' (p.3). Focus on the core word 'habitat' (p.18, glossary) and discuss what this means. Demonstrate how this core word, plus its prefixes and the suffix, form the word. How many different words can children make from the word 'habitat'? ('inhabit', 'habitable', 'uninhabitable', 'uninhabited', 'habitation', 'inhabited', 'inhabiting', 'inhabitable', 'inhabitation', 'inhabitant')

 ## Before reading

To activate prior knowledge and engage the reader

- Ask the children to look at their notes from Session I.
- Ask them what the 'It's Your Call' boxes are asking them to do. Why do they think the author has put in these boxes? **(deducing, inferring, drawing conclusions)**
- Tell them that they can select a spread to read from the rest of the book. Invite them to look at the contents page, then skim the spreads to select the spread they wish to read.
- Introduce the *It's Your Call summary* Photocopy Master so the children know that they will be making notes on this after they have read the spread.

During reading

- Ask the children to read their selected spread.
- Ask them to be aware of the main points the author is making.

....➤

> **Assessment point**
>
> Listen to individual children reading and make ongoing assessments on their decoding, sight vocabulary, approaches to tackling new words and their reading fluency. AF1

 ## After reading

Returning to the text

- Ask each child to sum up orally what their spread was about in a few sentences, and give their response to the 'It's Your Call' question, if they have one on their spread. **(summarizing, personal response)**

....➤

> **Assessment point**
>
> Can children interrogate the text, showing understanding and giving personal responses to it? AF2

Building comprehension

- Get the children to complete their summary sheet. Point out they will have to select the main idea and then some evidence to support it. Children can work in pairs if they have read the same spread. **(summarizing, determining importance)**

- Children could undertake further research on their chosen aspect using ICT and paper-based texts, and use appropriate features to locate information.
- They then prepare a brief presentation on their topic to give to the rest of the group.

Session 3 (pages 21–27)

 Before reading

To activate prior knowledge and engage the reader

- Ask the children to recap what they have read and noted to date. **(recall, summarizing)**
- Skim pages 21–27 together. Summarize the key argument on pages 20–23 (people are using more electricity and we are burning lots of non-renewable fuels to make this electricity. The gases released cause problems). **(summarizing)**
- Then look at the section on alternative power sources on pages 24–27. Point out how the pros and cons of each form of energy production are listed on page 26.
- Point out any difficult or technical vocabulary and check that children understand it.

 During reading

- Ask the children to read pages 24–27.
- As they read, ask them to notice the different ways pages 24 and 25, and pages 26 and 27 are presented.

> **Assessment point**
>
> Listen to individual children reading and make ongoing assessments on their decoding, sight vocabulary, approaches to tackling new words and their reading fluency. **AF1**

 After reading

Returning to the text

- Ask the children to name some sources of renewable energy and give examples of how energy can be saved in the home. **(recall)**

Building comprehension

- Ask each pair of children to select a renewable energy – one child argues for its use, while the other argues against its use. They should use the chart on page 26 to prepare their arguments. **(determining importance, synthesizing)**

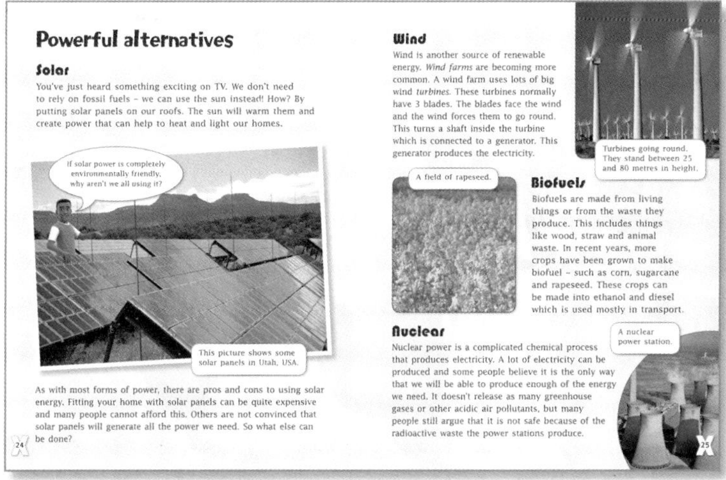

Follow-up activities

Writing activities

- Using any notes they have made on their *It's Your Call summary* Photocopy Master, their oral debates and information in the pro/cons charts from the book (p.14–15, 19 and 26) ask children to select the topic that most interests them and write a discussion text, using the *It's Your Call writing frame* Photocopy Master, if required. **(long writing task)**

- Create a recycling checklist for the classroom. **(short writing task)**

- Create a 'Saving energy (or water) in our school' poster. **(short writing task)**

Cross-curricular and thematic opportunities

- Compose a jingle to encourage people to recycle. Add movements if possible. Perform it to other classes. **(Music)**

- Undertake a survey of how people travel to school. Chart the results. **(Maths, Geography)**

- Research the concept of 'walking buses' (see www.walkingbus.com). Discuss the feasibility of setting up a 'walking bus' in your school. **(ICT, PSHE)**

The Witness

BY JOANNA NADIN

	Literacy Framework objective	Target and assessment focus
Speaking, listening, group interaction and drama	o Offer reasons and evidence for their views, considering alternative opinions 1.1 o Respond appropriately to the contributions of others in the light of differing viewpoints 1.2	o We can debate decisions, listening to and responding to different views on these **AF3**
Reading See also continuous reading objectives listed on page 9.	o Deduce characters' reasons for behaviour from their actions 7.2 o Explain how writers use figurative and expressive language to create images and atmosphere 7.5	o We can explain what characters' actions tell us about their character **AF3** o We can identify where authors have used special language and explain its impact **AF5**

The following notes provide a structure for four guided/group reading sessions. They are intended to be used flexibly; you may choose to focus on all four sessions or you could focus on one session and have the children read the rest of the book independently. In Session 1, children will read up to page 14. Children will read pages 15 to 29 in Session 2, Session 3 focuses on pages 30 to 41 and children will read pages 42 to the end in Session 4.

Session 1 (Saturday, Sunday)

 **Before reading**

To activate prior knowledge and encourage prediction

- Introduce the book, look at the front cover and discuss what kind of writing they would expect to find in a diary (personal details, first person account written soon after the event, frank, informal language). Whose diary is this? What do the children think will be recorded in the diary? **(predicting)**

To introduce new vocabulary

- Quickly skim the chapters *Saturday* and *Sunday*, asking children to identify any unusual words, e.g. *diabetes* (p.5).

 **During reading**

- Ask the children to read the first two chapters. If they encounter new vocabulary, ask them to use their dictionaries to explore the meanings of these words.
- Ask the children what to do if they encounter a difficult word, modelling with an example from the book.

> **Assessment point**
>
> Listen to individual children reading and make ongoing assessments on their decoding, sight vocabulary, approaches to tackling new words and their reading fluency. AF1

 **After reading**

Returning to the text

Saturday

- Why is BAD in capital letters? **(inferring, deducing)**
- What evidence is there that the Parrys are often involved in bullying? **(drawing conclusions)**

Sunday

 Why did the Parrys come to Eddie's house? **(inferring, deducing)**

- How did Eddie react? What does this tell us about his character? **(recalling, drawing conclusions)**

- Why do the Parrys give Eddie a nickname?

- Why do the children think some of the chapter is written as a diary?

Building vocabulary

- Explore the homophones noted in the vocabulary chart on page 11, listing all the alternatives. Use them in sentences.

- Make themed word collections (illness words or fear words).

Session 2 (Monday, Tuesday)

Before reading

To activate prior knowledge and encourage prediction

 Ask the children to recap the story to date and discuss how various characters are feeling. Discuss the author's style (see Session 1) and any humour or language play. What do they think will happen next? **(predicting)**

To introduce new vocabulary

- Quickly skim chapters *Monday* and *Tuesday*, asking children for the meaning and pronunciation of any unusual words, e.g. *collage*.

During reading

- Ask the children to read these chapters.

- Ask them to think about the characters' actions and what this tells them about the character. **(deducing, inferring, drawing conclusions)**

Assessment point
Can children explain what the characters are like by what they do and say? AF3

After reading

Returning to the text

Monday

 How does Eddie react to Sean's appeal? Why? What does this tell us about his character? **(recalling, inferring, drawing conclusions)**

 Why do you think the Parrys gave Eddie the computer game? **(deducing)**

- What evidence is there that Eddie knows he should not be doing what he's doing? **(drawing conclusions, synthesizing)**

Tuesday

- How does Eddie become more deeply involved in the bullying?

- Do you think Miss Hicks suspects about the bullying? Why? (pages 27 and 29) **(deducing, inferring)**

Building comprehension

- Use the *I think, I say, I feel* Photocopy Master to illuminate moments in the story when Eddie thinks one thing but does another or has to hide his real feelings.

Session 3 (Wednesday, Thursday)

Before reading

To activate prior knowledge and encourage prediction

- Ask the children to recap the story to date, discuss how various characters are feeling and ask them to predict what they think will happen next. **(activating prior knowledge, predicting)**

To engage readers and support fluent reading

- Invite one or two children to read some of the book aloud. Praise expressive reading, saying how it was expressive.

During reading

 Ask the children to read chapters *Wednesday* and *Thursday*.

After reading

Returning to the text

Wednesday

- What happens to Sean and how does Eddie react? **(recall)**

- Do you think Eddie was brave to tell the Parrys he wasn't going to be involved anymore? **(personal response)**

- Why do the Parrys use the watching sign and make chicken noises? **(inferring, deducing)**

Thursday

- Why and how does Eddie lie to his dad? **(recall)**
- How is he feeling? **(inferring, deducing)**

Building comprehension

- Are there any positive aspects of the Parrys' character? **(critical stance)**
- What do we know or can work out about Eddie's relationship with his father? **(deducing, drawing conclusions)**

Building fluency

- Create play scripts for any of the chapters. Include dialogue, stage directions and actions for the characters. Perform these scripts.
- After the performance return to the chapter and reread it aloud using lots of expression for the dialogue.

Session 4 (Friday, Saturday)

 **Before reading**

To activate prior knowledge and encourage prediction

- Ask the children to recap the story to date, discuss how various characters are feeling and get them to predict what they think will happen next. **(activating prior knowledge, predicting)**

 **During reading**

- Ask the children to read chapters *Friday* and *Saturday*.
- As they read ask them to be thinking about the characters' actions and what this tells them about the character. **(deducing, inferring, drawing conclusions)**

 **After reading**

Returning to the text

Friday

- How does Eddie's dad react when he finds the game? **(recall)**
- What does Eddie do that is very brave? **(recall)**
- How does the headteacher respond to the situation? **(recall)**

Saturday

- Are the Parrys punished, helped, or both? **(recall)**
- How do we know Sean forgives Eddie? **(inferring)**
- What lesson has Eddie learned? **(drawing conclusions)**

Building comprehension

- Identify references to food and eating. How does the author use food to add to our understanding of how the characters are feeling? **(synthesizing, inferring, deducing, drawing conclusions)**
- Ask the children to identify how the author uses imagery on page 44 (stroking like you would stroke a cat). How does this help the reader? **(visualizing)**

Follow-up activities

Writing activities

- Write diary entries for Sean after The Hut incident (first *Saturday* chapter) and the lunch money incident (*Tuesday*). **(short writing task)**
- Use the *What are they saying* Photocopy Master to add speech bubbles to the 'cartoon strip' from page 53. **(short writing task)**
- Use the *Nicknames* Photocopy Master to list the nicknames in the book. What do children think of the characters' nicknames? Can they create nicknames for people in the class? Discuss why cruel nicknames are not allowed. **(ongoing)**

Other literacy activities

- Debate whether the Parrys need punishment, help, or both. Children must justify their opinion and listen respectfully to others' opinions. **(speaking and listening)**

Cross-curricular and thematic opportunities

- Discuss and create a class checklist of bullying behaviour. For example, would children include verbal behaviour such as name calling, gestures and so on? Discuss what actions to take if children are bullied or witness bullying. **(PSHE)**
- Create 'Say NO to bullying' posters. **(PSHE/Art)**

A Matter of Life and Death

BY MICK GOWAR

	Literacy Framework objective	Target and assessment focus
Speaking, listening, group interaction and drama	o Offer reasons and evidence for their views, considering alternative opinions 1.1 o Respond appropriately to the contributions of others in the light of differing viewpoints 1.2	o We can debate decisions, listening to and responding to different views on these **AF3**
Reading See also continuous reading objectives listed on page 9.	o Explain how ideas are developed in non-fiction texts 7.2 o Read extensively ... genres and experiment with other types of texts 8.1	o We can explain how ideas are developed in non-fiction texts **AF2** o We can read and recognize a range of genres including mixed genre texts **AF4**

The following notes provide a structure for one to three guided/group reading sessions. They are intended to be used flexibly; you may choose to focus on one section in the book only, follow the suggestions for that section, and have the children read the rest of the book independently. Alternatively, you may choose to focus on the three sections in three guided/group reading sessions.

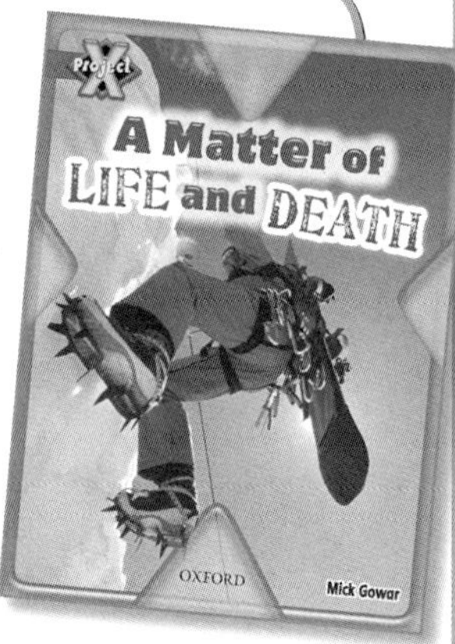

Session 1 (William Bligh), pages 5–9)

 ### Before reading

To activate prior knowledge and encourage prediction

- Read the section about Captain Bligh on page 2. Ask the children to consider what dilemmas and decisions might face Captain Bligh. Discuss what his 'life or death' situation is. **(deducing, inferring, predicting)**

To introduce new vocabulary

- Quickly skim the section and identify any new or challenging vocabulary. Discuss the meaning and pronunciation of these words.

 ### During reading

- Ask the children to read the section.
- Ask the children what to do if they encounter a difficult word, modelling with an example from the book if necessary.

 ### After reading

Returning to the text

- Why did the crew mutiny? **(recall)**
- Why did Bligh beg for his sextant, charts and papers? **(recall)**
- Why didn't Bligh go to the nearest islands? **(recall)**

Building comprehension

- The text says Bligh was a superb navigator. Is this fact or opinion? What is the evidence? **(inferring, deducing)**
- Discuss what the experience of spending 47 days in such a small space (9 metres x 2 metres) must feel like. **(emphathizing)**

- In the contemporary account, the sailors have 'tears of joy and gratitude flowing'. Who were they grateful to? **(inferring, deducing)**

Building vocabulary

- Explore the homophones noted in the vocabulary chart on page 11, listing all the alternatives and using these in sentences to show their meaning.

- Make word family collections based on new vocabulary, such as: explore, explorers, exploration.

Session 2 (Alexander Selkirk, pages 10–17)

Before reading

To activate prior knowledge and encourage prediction

- Read the section about Alexander Selkirk on page 2. Ask the children to consider what dilemmas and decisions Alexander Selkirk might face. What is his 'life or death' situation? **(deducing, inferring, predicting)**

To engage readers and support fluent reading

- Read aloud the opening paragraph on page 10, using your voice to build excitement and tension.

During reading

- Ask the children to read the section.
- As they read, ask them to think about the main protagonist's actions and the decisions he made. What does this tell the reader about his character?

After reading

Returning to the text

- Why was Selkirk living alone on the island? **(recall)**
- What was the important decision Selkirk made? **(recall)**
- How did he use what he had with him to survive? **(recall)**

Building comprehension

- Shelter, food and clothing are essential to humans. How did Selkirk cope with each of these needs? **(synthesizing)**
- What words describe Selkirk's feelings when he was left on the island? Ask children to imagine how he felt describing these feelings. **(empathizing)**

Session 3 (Ernest Shackleton, pages 18–24)

 **Before reading**

To activate prior knowledge and encourage prediction

- Read the section about Ernest Shackleton on page 3 to the children. Ask the children to consider what kinds of dilemmas and decisions might occur for him. What is his 'life or death' situation? **(deducing, inferring, predicting)**

To introduce new vocabulary

- Quickly skim the section and identify any new or challenging vocabulary. Discuss the meaning and pronunciation of these words.

 **During reading**

- Ask the children to read the section.
- As they read, ask them to think about Shackleton's actions and decisions. What does this tell the reader about his character?

 **After reading**

Returning to the text

- What decision did Shackleton make in December 1914? What do you think influenced Shackleton's decision? **(deducing)**
- Why did most of the men stay behind on Elephant Island? **(recall)**
- What obstacles did Shackleton overcome to get from Elephant Island to the fishing village on South Georgia? **(recall)**

Building comprehension

- What leadership qualities did Shackleton show? **(inferring, deducing, drawing conclusions)**
- Look at the pictures of the men, their environment and their equipment. Describe the qualities needed to survive this adventure? **(empathizing)**

Follow-up activities

Writing activity

- Compare Bligh and Shackleton's journeys. What skills and qualities did both men share? **(short writing task)**

Other literacy activities

- Debate whether Shackleton was very brave or very foolish. Ask children to back up their opinions with evidence. **(speaking and listening, personal response, adopting a critical stance)**

- Create a radio programme of any of the adventures stressing the life and death decisions that each man made. **(speaking and listening)**

- Look at the range of genres within this book (chronological recounts, lists, personal accounts, explanations, instructions and mixed genres). Explore the language features and grammar of any of these.

- Undertake the problem-solving activity on pages 14 and 15. **(speaking and listening)**

Cross-curricular and thematic opportunities

- Use the Internet to research what happened to the mutineers and Bligh once Bligh got back to England. **(ICT)**
- Undertake the instructional activity on page 9. **(Science, DT)**
- Find the Juan Fernandez Islands in an atlas or a world map using the information given on page 10. Using the atlas or map create a sea route back from the island to Scotland. **(Geography)**
- Create freeze frames of Shackleton's journey showing all the hazards. Add a musical sound track. **(Drama, Music)**
- Create a board for the game described on pages 26–27 and play the game. Make an instruction leaflet. **(Maths, DT)**